Wait...Who Got Goosed?®
Vol. 2

Wait...Who Got Goosed?®

Vol. 2

**MORE Mother Goose Rhymes Revisited...
Not for Sippy Cup, Booster Seat,
Thumb-sucking Young'uns**

Julie Coles

Wait...Who Got Goosed?™ Vol. 2: More Mother Goose Rhymes Revisited...
Not for Sippy Cup, Booster Seat, Thumb-sucking Young'uns
Julie Coles

Published by Pivot In New Directions Publishing®

Library of Congress Control Number 2025917805

ISBN (hardcover): 978-1-954912-19-9
ISBN (paperback): 978-1-954912-11-3
ISBN (eBook): 978-1-954912-21-2
ISBN (audiobook): 978-1-954912-22-9

POE005010 POETRY / American / General

Copyeditor: Lisa Shrewsberry
Proofreader: Madison McMillion
Book Designer: Michelle M. White, MMW Books
Illustrator, Whitney Marshall, WMarshall Designs
Project Manager: Talya Marshall

Warning: This book contains mild profanity.

Contact the author at
ImagineAMorePromisingFuture.com

Table of Contents

Chapter 1   **Truly Inexplicable Moments**   1

I'll Have More of Whatever That Was   3

Hazards of Daylight Savings Time   5

A Chilling Moment On A Chilly Morning   7

Chapter 2   **What Exasperation Looks Like**   9

The Life of an Underappreciated Queen   11

From Envy to Caution   14

Independent Joan   16

Not So Merry Mary   17

Predictably Unpredictable Forecasts   19

Chapter 3   **Some Driven to Inspire...**   21

Snow on the Ground Confounds Robins   23

Old Woman Living in a Shoe   24

Old Woman of Leeds   26

The King of France   27

Neat Little Clock   28

Chapter 4   **Others...Not So Much**   33

              Community Church Bells Communing   35
              Elsie Marley Is Quite Snarly   37

Chapter 5   **Useful Ways to Self Help**   41

              As I Walked by Myself   43
              Questionable Benefits of Keep Away Plans   44
              Pat-A-Cake   46
              One Two, Buckle My Shoe   47

Chapter 6   **Regrettable Decisions**   49

              Just How Nimble Is Jack?   51
              Little Boy in the Barn   52
              Tweedle-Dee and Not So Tweedle-Dumb   53

Chapter 7   **Audacious Women**   55

              The Consequence of Inseparable Bonds   57
              The Pumpkin-Eater   59
              When Resources Don't Match Aspirations   60

Acknowledgments   61

About the Author   63

CHAPTER 1
Truly Inexplicable Moments

I'll Have More of Whatever That Was

As I was walking in a field of wheat
I picked up something good to eat
What it was I couldn't exactly say
But I haven't tasted its like to this very day

I'm left with a memory, which I try to savor
Hoping for a chance to again taste the unique flavor
A distinct taste, unlike any I've ever known
With plant-like features different from any crops planted and grown

So delicate to the touch and, in my mouth, melting fast
With an abundance of the mysterious flavor, wanting its aftertaste
to last
Try as I might to give this unfathomable food a name
I retraced my steps to determine from where it came

I could only remember it was so aesthetically pleasing to the eye
It seemed to beckon me to come closer; I could not just pass it by
I plucked it from the ground, the only one there of its kind
Raising it gently towards my nose, conveying a message to my mind

"Taste me," it said, "I shall do you no harm. Go ahead, eat."
I succumbed without hesitation, rewarded with such a tasteful treat
Its after-effects were surprisingly gratifying
A spiritual metamorphosis overcame my being, for which there
was no denying

Blissfully, I stood absorbing this peaceful and tranquil state

An aphrodisiac quality about it tempted me to contemplate

What were its origins? Did the lovely plant have a name?

But I sensed, intuitively, that further research would be in vain

So there I was, enveloped, rendered motionless, yet at peace

Overcome with an awesome sense of well-being from which I did not seek release

Majestic moments elicited by rare foods are quite special to be sure

But they're made more beautiful if life's journey leads you to moments so pure.

Hazards of Daylight Savings Time

Hickory, dickory, dock!

The mouse ran up the clock;

The clock struck one,

Signaling it was time to get into some mischievous fun

But it was daylight savings time, and the clock hadn't yet been reset—

The homeowner was still at home basking in the sun, idly sitting on the back deck

Assuming it was all clear, the entire community of mice emerged without concern

Casually proceeding to their favorite hang-out spots, for which they did yearn

Especially after long weekends trapped inside their cubby holes for three days straight

'Twas an endurance test of avoiding traps laced with the most delicious bait

Just a whiff of food set in mousetraps made the mice weak in the knees—

It was particularly challenging when traps were baited with their favorite—*very* Gouda cheese

Back to the present when, without warning, heavy footsteps came through the back door

Uh-Oh! The mice began to sweat, creating little mouse puddles all on the floor

Panicked with fright and the thought of being caught,

Every mouse froze in place, trapped in panic, overwhelmed by thought

Sure, they knew how to scamper away when their numbers were just one or a few,

But there were way too many to not be noticed now; they fretted over what to do

A scary moment subsided to instinct— they froze like statues in a museum

When, unexpectedly, the owner remembered his iced tea outside they improvised a new plan

Hearing the clink of the ice and the man sitting down, they turned, hightailed it to the basement

Out of breath and hearts pounding, relieved at how well their exodus went

Grabbing their mini handkerchiefs, they wiped the sweat from their furry little brows,

The young ones hi-fiving one another, confident they would always make it to safety somehow

Not the elders, so exhausted they thought it best to discuss the matter later

There were many erratic old mouse heartbeats that day,

But they were fortunate to have mini defibrillators.

A Chilling Moment On A Chilly Morning

One misty, moist morning,

When cloudy was the weather,

I chanced to see a man all clothed in leather.

He was toting a gun

So I turned, decided to haul ass, and began to run.

I snatched a look back; he was right on my heel.

Out of breath I stopped and asked, "Hey, what's the deal?"

It was to no avail because I got no reply,

And I kind of figured then and there I just might be about to die.

But I went ahead and continued my friendly approach.

"Why do you want to harm me? I'm just one of the common folks."

Still from him not a comment—

I mean zip, nada, not a thing.

So I paused a moment, and in my head a kind of bell did ring.

I politely asked, "How is it you came to be so mean?

After all, I was just struttin' along minding my business when you
entered scene."

And finally, I got a reaction, much to my surprise.

It actually brought a kind of twinkle to his devious eyes.

He mumbled ever so softly, "Chasing folks is so much fun.

It helps me to relieve my constant state of boredom."

I said, "Oooh I get it, yes, yes—now I understand."

Hoping my empathetic response would change the direction of the gun in his hand.

Nope. That didn't do it—I had only hoped in vain

because he grinned that eerie smile that signaled this dude is probably insane.

Without hesitation, I reached out and disarmed him, threw him up against the fence.

I yelled, "Find another outlet for your boredom, buster,

'cause it ain't fair to find joy in inflicting pain at other people's expense!"

CHAPTER 2
What Exasperation Looks Like

The Life of an Underappreciated Queen

The Queen of Hearts

She made some tarts

All on a summer's day

Over a hot stove

She sweated and grunted,

Insisting on doing things her way

Take the laundry, for instance,

She had a method

Tried and true

She instructed her family

To pay close attention

Demonstrating what they should do

In the basement were eight colored bins

Each numbered and decorated

To help tell them apart

"You'll undress down here

Putting clothes in marked barrels," she said,

Indicating where they should start...

The cooking and laundry were just the beginning

So many daily tasks to be done!

She, alone, had to oversee

Keeping track of the bills...

Calling her children's teachers
To ensure they achieved high grades—never less than a B

She also made time
For her elderly parents
In a nearby nursing home
And when she had some free time
She generously indulged herself
Taking strolls through the kingdom alone

With everything accomplished by day's end,
She'd be completely exhausted but fulfilled
She truly had earned her rest
So she fell into bed
Grasping and adjusting the pillow for her head
Whispering firmly to the King, "Honey, please remove your hand from my chest."

He had no appreciation
Not the least bit of understanding
For all the work she had done!
She was especially annoyed when he chided then pleaded
"I have missed you so much today...
Why can't we have just a little fun?"

She replied, "I've worked so hard
Keeping up with the kids is exhausting,
I'm doing everything possible to make *your* palace *our* home!"

Disgruntled and frustrated

He moved to the other side of the bed

And muttered, "Fine...maybe I'll start to roam."

"What did you say?"

She turned in anger, threatening an argument,

Which the King knew would soon become full-blown

"Oh nothing, sweet pea," he said

"I was just thinking out loud...

About my upcoming trip to Rome."

From Envy to Caution

Ever wonder what it's like to walk in the shoes
Of someone experiencing serious money blues?

If I'd as much money as I could spend
I just know it would bring my financial woes to a joyful end

Imagine all of my bills paid and no more debts hanging over my head!
I hear many with money invest in well-disguised tax shelters to fool the feds

I worry I could fall victim to the same cyclical wheel of dependency
Like so many unprepared overnight, get-rich folks, basking in euphoria-turned-misery

Rumors of lottery winners living hand-to-mouth
Digging deeply into pockets once bottomless, discovering their fingers couldn't reach further south

How did they get to that point with so much money to spend?
Were they plagued with greed and generosity, doling out inordinate sums to family and friends?

Perhaps they are unable to say, "No," when encroached upon by wannabes
Especially folks making polite conversation ending with the word "...please."

Or how about those who claim, "Oh you remember me, we met some time ago...

Sure you do, honey. I'm your distant cousin five times removed from your aunt's sister so and so."

Independent Joan

Here I am, little jumping Joan;

Even when with others,

I always feel alone.

"But why," people asked, "do you play alone all day?"

Joan quietly replied, "'Cause I prefer it that way."

"But don't you want comfort and companionship from others?"

"Are you kidding?!" she exclaimed. "I come from a household of eight sisters, nine brothers!"

"Is that the same as you choosing to be with your very own friends?"

"Nah, but it beats the heck out of constantly sharing or compromising."

And, with that, the conversation came to an end.

Not So Merry Mary

Mistress Mary, quite contrary

How does your garden grow?

Well, I don't normally reveal my secrets

But a combination of ingredients

Always enriches the soil

Of course, the fertilizer used is cow dung

Which I highly recommend, even if whiffing it ain't fun

I used to go out every other day to till the soil

But a massive spill has left my garden overrun with petroleum oil!

My vegetables are all lost; I especially miss my beautiful
flowerbeds

I posted horrific photos of many lifeless creatures I found

Lovely birds, now dead

Trying to keep up with those awful news reports is driving me
insane!

My neighbors and I call the officials every day to complain

Finally, a company rep inspected the neighborhood

And assured everyone that everything would be all good

They presented a cleanup plan and promised it would soon be fine

Several weeks passed with no action...

And responses to our messages were anything but kind

Eventually, no one took responsibility

The clean-up was left to my neighbors and me

Walking through my garden is now unpleasant,

With so much decay on the ground

I wear an oxygen mask and waist-high boots just to get around

You should've seen the variety of vegetables I once sold at the

Flea Market on Saturdays!

Crops impacted by the spill don't appeal

To buyers who now walk by loudly muttering, "No way!"

Even my dog, Fido, slides on rubber boots to go out to take a pee

Because he's no longer fond of taking care of his business

Near contaminated bushes and trees!

Predictably Unpredictable Forecasts

A sun-shiny shower
Won't last a half an hour

But that likely depends on your location—
Meteorologists aren't sure what forecasts to give—
And this fills them with much consternation

The fluctuation in weather patterns absolutely drives them nuts
Advising viewers to pack raincoats and umbrellas while predicting blue skies,
Their reports always end with a cautious bouquet of "Buts..."

Exasperated from so much uncertainty,
Families sunbathing feel particularly annoyed when rain suddenly arrives, causing a calamity
Heading back from the beach, they utter their displeasure laced with a bit of profanity

Ahhh... but on those nice days when the meteorologist is your very best friend
Pocket some of that sunshine for future bad forecasts as a reminder
That, good or bad, all weather will eventually come to an end

CHAPTER 3

Some Driven to Inspire...

Snow on the Ground Confounds Robins

The little robin grieves
When the snow is on the ground
For the trees have no leaves
And no berries or worms can be found

Being tenacious and resilient
They each find ways to survive
Despite nature's seasonal changes
We all discover an ability to thrive

When finding food becomes a challenge
Persistent hunger overcomes giving in
That's when our feathered friends, like us,
Discover the fortitude to survive...and win

Old Woman Living in a Shoe

There was an old woman who lived in a shoe

She had so many children, she didn't know what to do.

After several years of asking around

Her friends referred her to the Welfare Office in town.

She said to the clerk, "Food stamps is what I need,

After all, as you may know, I've got so many mouths to feed."

She was told to take a number and stand in the long line.

She glared at the clerk and said, "But I ain't got that much time!"

While she walked away she mumbled to herself,

"The lottery is probably a quicker way to earn wealth."

Hearing her number called, she stomped to the door and gave it a tap.

Someone opened a window, and she said, "I'm here to apply for SNAP!"

She strutted into the office and threw down her bag.

Not the least intimidated, the clerk welcomed the woman, who many unfairly referred to as "old nag."

Hearing that she was caring for several orphans while living in a shoe,

This kind clerk gave her a warm smile and stated, "Let's see what we can do."

Surprised by the gesture of kindness and respect,

The old woman's demeanor changed, mystified by behavior contrary to what she had come to expect.

The clerk said, "We'll need to follow the procedures, that is
the norm.

The services could take some time to begin after we fill out
these forms."

Feeling embarrassed to admit she couldn't read or write,

The old woman became defensive which triggered a desire to
take flight.

Sensing the woman's apprehension, the clerk filled the silence by
reading each section aloud,

Then asked her if she needed more clarification, wanting to
maintain the woman's dignity and right to be proud.

There is an old woman who used to live in a shoe.

She and the kids moved into the condo on Linden Street; I believe
it's #202

Old Woman of Leeds

There was an old woman of Leeds,

Who spent all her time doing good deeds;

She worked for the poor

At the shelter next door

And she gave of herself tirelessly

Working long days, 5 until 3

She kept things clean and tidy

Leaving workers amazed

At how her stamina seemed to never fade

When asked how, she replied, "You're welcome to follow me!"

The King of France

The King of France went up the hill

With twenty thousand men

The King of France returned with less than half of his fleet

Vowing to never go up that hill again

Left bereft and horrified by the consequence of going to war

After witnessing the slaying and senseless loss of loyal citizens

He wondered aloud, "What was I sacrificing so many lives for?"

One of his lieutenants yelled, "We did it for honor and pride, my great king!"

Upon which a cacophony of cheers arose with fists in the air

The teary-eyed leader felt fighting for pride and honor was such a hollow thing

The next day, he declared his nation would participate in war no more

Making clear his citizens' lives were no less valuable than his own

His citizens agreed, posting funeral notices of fallen loved ones on their doors

Hopes of never again being put in calamitous and unwarranted disputes

Threatening the independence of sovereign nations

A global peace treaty was created

No country would ever overtake another to satisfy one's selfish need for ego elevation

Neat Little Clock

There's a neat little clock

In the schoolroom it stands

As students arrive to class, someone unfamiliar gives a welcome

Then begins spouting commands

"Now, class, we've much to cover

So open up your history books.

There are many misrepresentations and inaccurate assertions—

Why don't we all take a look?"

Her comments grabbed each student's attention

Everyone anxious to confirm what they'd just heard

We all straightened up in our seats

While feeling a bit skeptical, wondering if she were just being
absurd

For students, most school days are uneventful and so boring

Information delivered in a style that feels unimportant and
mundane

But this particular class hinted that somehow it might be different

'Cause this teacher's perspective was interesting (maybe even a
bit insane)

Her opening statements encouraged us

To question much of whatever we read

And to not put all of our faith in the reporters

Who announce the news on T.V.

This really turned our room into utter chaos

Whispers flying here and there

What might come out of her mouth next?

None could say, we were completely unaware!

True, we were in school to learn a great deal

To open our minds to the unknown, and become more enlightened

But what she said dramatically shifted our assumptions

Eyebrows raised, mouths agape, some of us feeling apprehensive and a tad bit frightened

She began to give us examples

About some truths that were hidden behind many lies

About how Abe Lincoln freed, yet continued to own slaves

Leaving many like us to ponder, "Why?"

We also learned many new words

Which greatly enhanced our vocabulary

Insisting that we understand the connection of terms like "contradiction" and "hypocrite"

Because they factor into the fabric of America's true history

Like Columbus who was to have sailed across the ocean

And credited for discovering America in 1492

But in truth, he proclaimed a land already occupied by Native American Indians

Subjected to degradation and confined to reservations—the research showed this to be true

She scanned the faces in the class, searching our eyes

While tapping a number two lead pencil against her knee

Sensing our attentiveness as we sat mesmerized

She cheerfully asked, "Is everyone still with me?"

We consumed a lot of mind-boggling information

In what seemed too short of a time span, just short of an hour

When the bell rang to signal the end of the class, no one budged

Because this extraordinary messenger spoke so eloquently and with
such power

The school was abuzz and we were amazed

Finally our education mattered, and we really began to care

Each of our minds and hearts were completely invested

We couldn't wait to bring what we had experienced in class home
to share

And bring it home we did, such enthusiastic but naive kids

As our parents listened, their faces gradually showed signs of alarm

After asking probing questions they immediately called our school

Protesting that our new History teacher was wreaking havoc and
causing potential harm

Unbeknownst to us there was such a great fuss

As we made our way back to room four-oh-three

Wouldn't you know it? The rumors were true

Another teacher stood at the front of the room holding just one book
and said, "Let's get busy!"

Too young to understand the consequences of being misunderstood,

To us, the fate of our previous teacher was a complete mystery

Whether she was fired or as the principal suggested, retired,

The news unsettled everyone fortunate enough to have experienced something so extraordinary

Her replacement took an all-too-familiar stance

Imploring us to take the written words at face value

In no time we returned to daydreaming or watching the clock

Then home to genuinely pleased parents excitedly asking, "Hey, how was school?"

I replied, "Boring 'cause I kept losing my concentration,

Especially in History, where I didn't retain a thing

Taught strictly by the book, without so much as a second look

We just kept staring at the clock, waiting for the class bell to ring!"

"Cheer up," they said, "things will get better."

Tossing me a smile and a loving wink

But I greeted their optimism with pessimism

'Cause they hadn't experienced this teacher who had inspired us to think

CHAPTER 4
Others...Not So Much

Community Church Bells Communing

Ahhh... the familiar sound of church bells ringing!

They may inspire thoughts of prayer, sermons, or singing—

But have you ever wondered about the sequence of multiple chimes?

If they were attempting to communicate with one another just what might be on their minds?

What religious institutions withhold from the public domain—

Surreptitious facts from social media fiction—

Is absolutely insane!

So, perhaps conflicts are revealed in the ringing of bells to the fold,

Resolving issues among themselves through the use of clandestine code.

It's helpful to avoid contentious topics face-to-face;

Subjects become prickly when diverse participants occupy the same space.

Take, for example, the exchange or borrowing of funds—

Perhaps the chiming of bells represents debts owed to the people, in insurmountable sums.

One *chime code* successfully decoded may read:

You owe me five shillings,

Said the bells of St. Hillings.

When will you pay me?

Asked the bells of St. Baily.

Won't be any time soon,

Replied the bells of St. Buffoon.

Elsie Marley Is Quite Snarly

Elsie Marley thinks she's grown so fine

With such a high opinion of herself, believing it's okay to be unkind

Points contrary to her position, to her, are crossing the line

Elsie embraces life as a contrarian, believing she is right all of the time

Generally, adults are entitled to make their own decisions about life

But, if you reside near highly opinionated folks like Elsie, there's sure to be strife

Installation of high fences by nearby neighbors thinking separation would be nice

Only infuriated Elsie, who dismissed all boundaries; barriers of any kind never sufficed

Imposing her beliefs and will on others was her personality

Her parents have been terrified since her birth (she was such a terrifically fussy baby!)

Guardrails were useless, since they hindered her ability to live free

Ironically, Elsie's adult freedoms only caused others misery

Elsie's a vegetarian, proclaiming loudly her distaste of meat from pork on down to fish

Naturally, she's intolerant of consumers eating foods clearly forbidden on her own dish

The inability to eat at restaurants offending her olfactory senses

Makes her jealous of the fun being missed,

Which elevates her outrage, immediately adding new grievances to her grievance list

She even launched a scare campaign touting the hazards of eating certain fare

Complete with AI images so professional, they had many fooled and unaware

She succeeded in banding the community together to boycott the local grocer

Did it matter that the information was skewed with gross misrepresentations? No Sir!

Check out her meetings from 7 to 9 every Monday night

You'll identify her easily; she's the one with the overbite

Occupying the only seat on stage under a spotlight

She succeeds in creating the spectacle of an intimidating and authoritarian sight

She begins each meeting with a bang of the fist

Then shouts her latest demands, all unilaterally decided by her on the list

Oh, it's usually the same old thing

Which, by now, has an all too familiar ring

"Please refrain from purchasing this, that, and the other."

One foolish townie ignored the boycotts despite pleas from the townie's mother

So with Elsie the townspeople met

Proclaiming profusely that they were quite upset

When—wouldn't you just know it?—this ignorant townie decided to show

And as you might imagine, the community's hostility began to grow

Her presence created such a calamity

Within the first few minutes, outrage led to threats laced with profanity

Typically, encounters such as this never reach an amicable solution

Especially when Elsie's spewing turns to righteous indignation for a social revolution

In the end, the community decided to ostracize the ignorant one

Resulting in a town filled with so much resentment, no one had much fun

Particularly the local grocer, who had to pack up her shop

Forcing foreclosure—will the madness ever stop?

Ms. Elsie was pleased with herself; a victory had been won

Her vision of a new social order had, in her mind, successfully begun

She continued her regular rampages, leading to foreclosures all over town

Her Monday meetings are attended by few, 'cause there's scarcely anyone around

Most folks had to leave to pursue employment elsewhere

Leaving Elsie to bask in the joy of her lone revolution, about which nobody (but her) cares

CHAPTER 5

Useful Ways to Self Help

As I Walked by Myself

As I walked by myself
And talked to myself
Myself said unto me,
"Look to thyself,
Take care of thyself,
But don't forget to just *be*—

Fear not the passion for life
Residing within your heart.
Shy not away from taking risks,
For clarity isn't always at hand;
Life has its share of ups and downs,
But you'll benefit greatly from open-mindedness.

Enjoy the things and people who make your heart smile.
Take a chance;
Have the courage to look at others with more than a glance—
You've much to learn from the experiences of those around you.
Wisdom can't find you in a safe bubble,
So look, touch, see, and feel outside of yourself, too
Your natural instincts and connection to others will both see you through."

Questionable Benefits of Keep Away Plans

Albert's tears and Melinda's fears
Will make them old before their older years

They don't seem compatible
Yet they stay together, which many find unfathomable

If they stay together
How will they combat future storms most couples have to weather?

Can't imagine they'll experience much joy in their lives if they
don't get support
Once asked if they considered counseling, an emphatic "Nope"
was their retort

Despite future years of tears and fears being a continued burden
on family and friends
Albert and Melinda deployed *Keep Away Plans* to avoid faking
enjoyment and playing pretend

Over time, they eventually noticed the absence of those they truly
loved
Even the rare invitation they extended for get-togethers were met
with disinterested shrugs

Deciding to discard the *Keep Away Plans* initially filled them with
trepidation
But after a while it felt worth the risk, taking pleasure in
experiences that awakened them to new sensations

Apparently, people can influence the decisions of others in unexpected ways...

Albert and Melinda daily convey appreciation to others they no longer need to persuade to stay

Contending with the *hangers-on'ers* who over-stay their visits is a bit complicated

But discovered asking if they're in need of a ride service works when politely communicated

Pat-A-Cake

Pat-a-cake, pat-a-cake, baker's man

Why folks still use ovens and stoves

I just can't understand

We live in times where things can be made so quick

There's no need to slave over a stove

Especially if your culinary skills are susceptible of sometimes making others sick

With the advent of microwaves and other technology

There's no more hovering over hot stoves and ovens

This high-tech revolution has completely set me free!

I've grown accustomed, like so many others within our nation,

To no more waiting or much contemplating

When I can have instant gratification

So, the next time you want to pat-a-cake with your own, unskilled hand

Just stick that cake in the microwave or air fryer

And let it bake that bad boy faster, and better, than you can!

One Two, Buckle My Shoe

One, two
Tripping over my shoe

Three, four
Jammed my finger in the door

Five, six
My kid hid my lunch, just for kicks

Seven, eight
Pissed off 'cause the kid's prank made me arrive to work late

Nine, ten
Boss yells, "You're tardy again!"

Eleven, twelve
Muttered to my boss to go... take a sip from a well

Thirteen, fourteen
Came home to my spouse saying, "You're mean!"

Fifteen, sixteen
...saying, "The kid was only joking and was it really necessary to
cause such a scene?"

Seventeen, eighteen
Found myself wishing the events of the day were only a dream

Nineteen, twenty

In the middle of the spat was asked, "What's so funny?"

Twenty-one, twenty-two

Casually and emotionlessly, replied, "Are you through?"

Twenty-three, twenty-four

Grabbed my coat and headed out the door

Twenty-five, twenty-six

Went to a local bingo game instead of alcohol for a fix

Twenty-seven, twenty-eight

'Cause today's my tenth year of sobriety, which I intend to celebrate

CHAPTER 6

Regrettable Decisions

Just How Nimble Is Jack?

Jack prided himself on being so nimble

Often bragged about being so quick

Until he accepted a dare, that is,

To jump over a candlestick

Apparently, he didn't jump high enough

His decision to take off from a low crouch

Caused his pants to catch on fire

His agony was heard throughout the neighborhood, as he screamed, "Ouch! Ouch! Ouch!"

Little Boy in the Barn

There was a little boy who went into a barn

To lay down and take a nap on some hay

A calf unexpectedly wandered out and spooked the boy

Who, suddenly awakened, jumped up and ran away

The calf called, "Hey! Where ya goin', ya little chickenshit?

Your bucket's full every day, while I only get a little sip?

You take all her milk and leave nothin' for me

And because of you, I probably won't grow much bigger by the time I'm three!"

Tweedle-Dee and Not So Tweedle-Dumb

Tweedle-Dum and Tweedle-Dee

Were two black birds sitting contentedly

Minding their own business in a tree came naturally for them

That was, until all of the shooting did begin!

It was hunting season, but they both forgot

Tweedle-Dee and -Dum got nicked in the ass with a shot

"What the *%#@!" -Dum squawked to -Dee

"Why the hell is the hunter aimin' at you and me?"

"Aren't they supposed to be hunting quail and pheasants?"

Suddenly more shots rang out, making the moment even more
unpleasant!

-Dee and -Dum were almost nicked in their tail and wing...

Glaring angrily at one another, both Tweedles knew they had to
do something

So, they conferred back and forth, reaching a mutual plan

Launching phase one of their retaliation, like drones deftly
locating the man

With no more to be said, they decided to play dead,

Patiently awaiting the arrival of their main target: the hunter's
head

Timing was imperative to accomplishing this little trick

So, when he arrived at a certain spot, they poured it on thick—

Shit came dropping down from the tree

Causing the befuddled hunter to flee

But the hunter should have completed what he started and shot them dead

'Cause they continued the chase while dropping bird-bombs on top of his head

Yes, Tweedle-Dee and Tweedle-Dum

Managed to forget about their wounds, they were having so much fun

All the other birds chirped wildly and soon took flight

They, too, hated hunting season, hearing some human ate Cousin Levi for dinner last night

They also took aim and strategically dropped their load

Bombarding any hunter within sight, or that's what I've been told

You should have seen all of those grown men scampering out of the woods

Panting and cussing while vowing never to hunt again in that neighborhood!

Tweedle-Dum and Tweedle-Dee

Returned to their favorite perch up in the tree

Wait! Who's that? Another potential victim?

No—this one carried a sign, with hammer and nails—no gun

He posted the new sign, nearly wearing out his wrist

It read: "Beware of vengeful birds. Hunt here at your own risk!"

CHAPTER 7

Audacious Women

The Consequence of Inseparable Bonds

Molly (my sister) and I had another falling out;
I'm feeling a bit embarrassed revealing what this one was about!

She loves coffee and I love tea
But that wasn't the only reason we couldn't agree...

So many differences exist between us
It takes so little to spark a fuss

As you might imagine, it's sometimes unbearable living under the same roof
Whenever we argue, the matter is never settled, even if one provides proof

Truthfully, this might sound a bit insane
But, in some odd way, we seem to enjoy inflicting each other with pain

Oh, did I fail to mention that we are identical twins?
Which might explain our inexplicable desire for each to always win

This may also come as a surprise, but we miss one another when we're apart
I think our sense of wholeness comes from possessing the other half of each other's heart

We understand the sheer exhaustion others feel when in our presence

To family and friends our arguments make absolutely no sense!

The combative behavior makes us unpleasant to be around

I'm really afraid I'll lose a couple of new friends I found

It's as if we were born inside an impenetrable fortress of our own,

Making other family members feel unwelcomed in their own home

But the upheaval that occurred when our parents suggested we should consider living in different places

Triggered one of those rare moments where we shared the exact same look on our faces—

In unison we shouted, "Are you for real? Of course we intend to live together!"

We're birds born of the same feather, destined to be tethered in sisterhood forever.

The Pumpkin-Eater

Peter, Peter, pumpkin-eater

Had a wife and couldn't keep her;

He put her in a pumpkin shell,

She blurted out, "Wait! What the hell?"

Wondering, "Is this what being 'kept' truly means today?"

Retribution for independence prevented women from having
any say

Well, this won't do, she thought. No, not one bit

Having been used to coveting her freedom, she threw an absolute fit

Demanding to be set free, she banged and shouted, "Let me out!"

Imprisonment was never what marriage was supposed to be about

Was being involuntarily sealed inside a cold, slimy shell

Her reward for loving someone, for whom she really fell?

Relationships can be complicated, at times, yes, quite complex

But locking your spouse up isn't even in the fine print of wedding
vow texts

So, unlock that pumpkin shell and let your wives be!

Then, give some thought to seeking counseling or some form of
therapy

Oh, and ditch the pumpkin shell immediately!

Restraining others also prevents you from being truly free

When Resources Don't Match Aspirations

I take no joy when my little old man and I bicker back and forth
Most disagreements usually involve the topic of money, of course

He asked me for money because as usual he had none,
And that's the way this argument had begun

I falsely claimed money in the prenuptials we signed before
marriage that were never legally approved
Somehow I managed to keep that a secret to avoid being sued

I wanted him to believe my bank account was full of money
'Cause I got more attention and loved it when he called me "Honey"

Having my own separate account is helpful in maintaining the
deception
It gives me the upper-hand whenever I need to influence his
perceptions

Recently, he's been talking about a family and kids
"You'll need a better-paying job to afford them," I tell him
Which serves as the perfect lid

In an instant, talk of raising children is completely shot down
'Cause we both know I'd be the only caregiver since he's never
around

Acknowledgments

Unorthodox thinking and humorous ideas, often articulated in off-the-cuff remarks, inspired my desire to write across a variety of genres. Mother Goose Rhymes, revisited and revised through a sometimes pensive, sometimes lighthearted lens, provided an ideal landscape. The joy of writing Wait...Who Got Goosed™ Vols. 1 and 2 affirmed my decision to pivot in new and different directions. Volume 1 is for young'uns. But this volume of new poems, Volume 2, is intended for adults. Writing each represented two separate journeys, and both were labors of love.

My aspiration of writing Wait...Who Got Goosed? ™ books was achieved with generous support from a network of truly talented and devoted individuals; I was honored to work with them. The opportunity to collaborate with seasoned professionals in publishing elevated my poetry and storytelling skills. I'm especially grateful for their bravery and willingness to take this journey with me—a novice writer of poetry storytelling.

I immensely enjoyed writing this version of Wait...Who Got Goosed?™ Vol. 2. But the real litmus test of determining success will be primarily based on how readers experience the book. If you yearn for opportunities to find relief from the responsibilities of adulting, then this book will be a great escape for you!

About the Author

Inspired by the opportunity to PIVOT In New Directions™, where educating others is explored through a variety of lenses, author Julie Coles departed from the formality of writing education books and scratched an itch to explore other genres. These explorations include poetry, fiction, and other content including posters and blogs. Never intending to completely leave education, Julie maintains an education network on her website: ImagineaMorePromisingFuture.com.

Advocacy is another of Julie's passions. Through her creation of the Humane Discount Network, Julie encourages businesses to consider providing discounts to customers enduring economic hardships. Leading by example, Julie recently reduced prices and posted sales for all merchandise in her own shop, https://pind-publishing.myshopify.com/collections/all .

Julie is driven by a need to assist those in need. In addition to imagining and developing inspiring creative projects, Julie is dedicated to humanitarian organizations preserving the welfare of others. She makes intentional annual contributions to worthy causes both locally and nationally.

www.ingramcontent.com/pod-product-compliance
Lightning Source LLC
Chambersburg PA
CBHW061716120626
46550CB00003B/1243